INTRODUCTION

The original Lil Pudgys art was created by Antoine Mingo. This Pudgy Pals coffee table book was illustrated by JM and designed and produced by Pudgy Amateur, an early supporter of the Pudgy Penguin community. It is not affiliated or endorsed by the Igloo Company.

Stay in touch - we loved to know which Lil Pudgys are your favorites, and why! Say hello at hellopudgypals@gmail.com.

These characters have been developed with the intention of licensing them for various purposes, and I am open to discussing potential licensing opportunities. If you are interested in exploring licensing options for these characters, please feel free to email hellopudgypals@gmail.com to discuss further details.

Let's waddle in...

Pudgy Penguins Website

Lil Pudgy Instagram

#91

#198

3

#795

4

#1952

#3657

#4002

#5815

#6368

#7640

#9477

#9669

#9747

#9914

15

#10263

#10302

GM
#10405

#10786

#10846

#11206

22

PUDGY
#12303

#12381

#12854

#12970

#13272

#13513

#14353

#14692

#14830

#15714

#15821

34

#15875

#16448

#16955

#17295

#17342

#17795

#17936

#18004

#18571

#18574

#18764

#19238

#19605

#19754

#20227

#20257

#20574

#20742

#20956

#21273

#21290

#21437

#21576